Ragdoll Cats

by Grace Hansen

Abdo
CATS
Kids

abdopublishing.com

Published by Abdo Kids, a division of ABDO, P.O. Box 398166, Minneapolis, Minnesota 55439.

Copyright © 2017 by Abdo Consulting Group, Inc. International copyrights reserved in all countries. No part of this book may be reproduced in any form without written permission from the publisher.

Printed in the United States of America, North Mankato, Minnesota.

102016

012017

 THIS BOOK CONTAINS RECYCLED MATERIALS

Photo Credits: Alamy, Animal Photography, iStock, Shutterstock, Thinkstock

Production Contributors: Teddy Borth, Jennie Forsberg, Grace Hansen

Design Contributors: Dorothy Toth, Laura Mitchell

Publisher's Cataloging in Publication Data

Names: Hansen, Grace, author.

Title: Ragdoll cats / by Grace Hansen.

Description: Minneapolis, Minnesota : Abdo Kids, 2017 | Series: Cats. Set 2 |
    Includes bibliographical references and index.

Identifiers: LCCN 2016944105 | ISBN 9781680809213 (lib. bdg.) |
    ISBN 9781680796315 (ebook) | ISBN 9781680796988 (Read-to-me ebook)

Subjects: LCSH: Ragdoll cats--Juvenile literature.

Classification: DDC 636.8/3--dc23

LC record available at http://lccn.loc.gov/2016944105

Table of Contents

Ragdoll Cats

The ragdoll cat earned its name for the way it becomes **limp** when picked up. This is no surprise, since these cats are very easygoing.

Ragdolls are large cats. Most weigh between 10 and 15 pounds (4.5 and 6.8 kg). Some can reach 20 pounds (9.1 kg) or more! Their fluffy coats make them look even bigger.

Ragdolls come in many color and **pattern** combinations. But all have markings on their faces, legs, or tails.

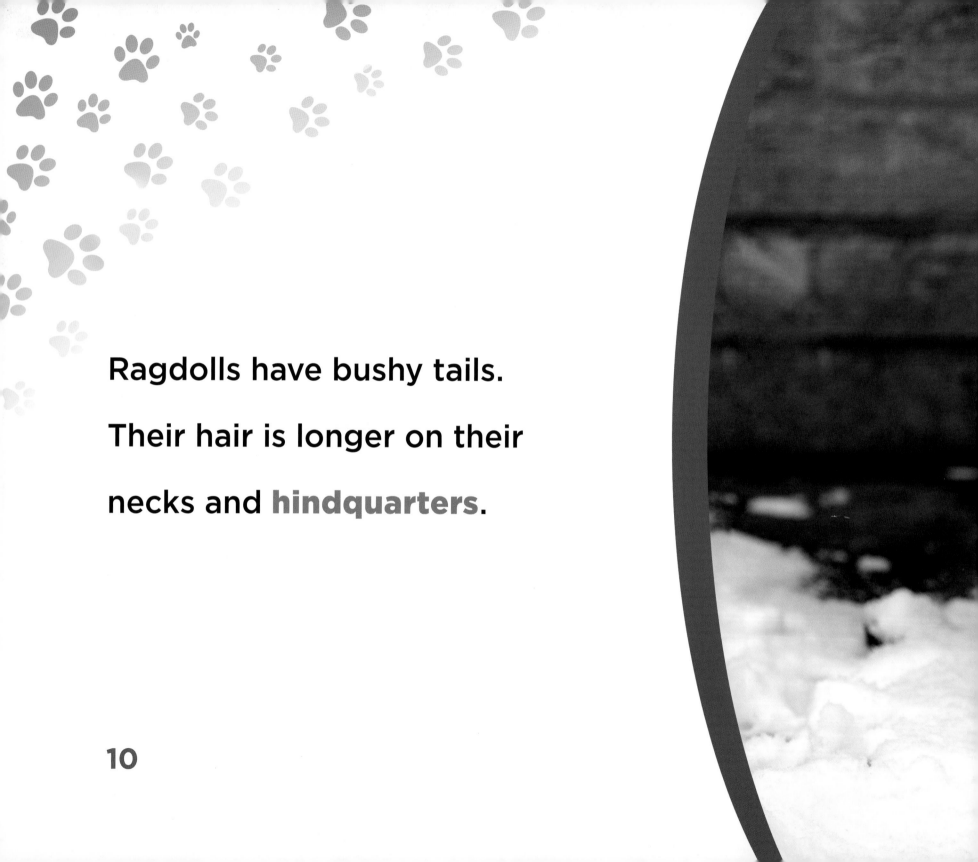

Ragdolls have bushy tails.

Their hair is longer on their

necks and **hindquarters**.

10

Ragdolls have bright blue eyes. Their small ears are pointed at the tips.

Grooming

Ragdolls shed, but not too much!
A good brushing three times a
week will help with shedding.
This also keeps the coat healthy!

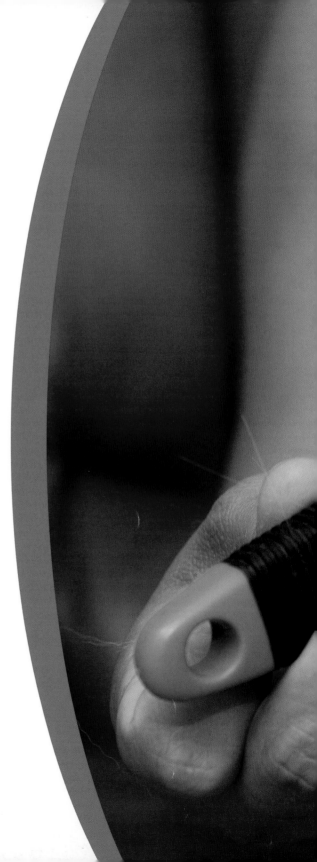

14

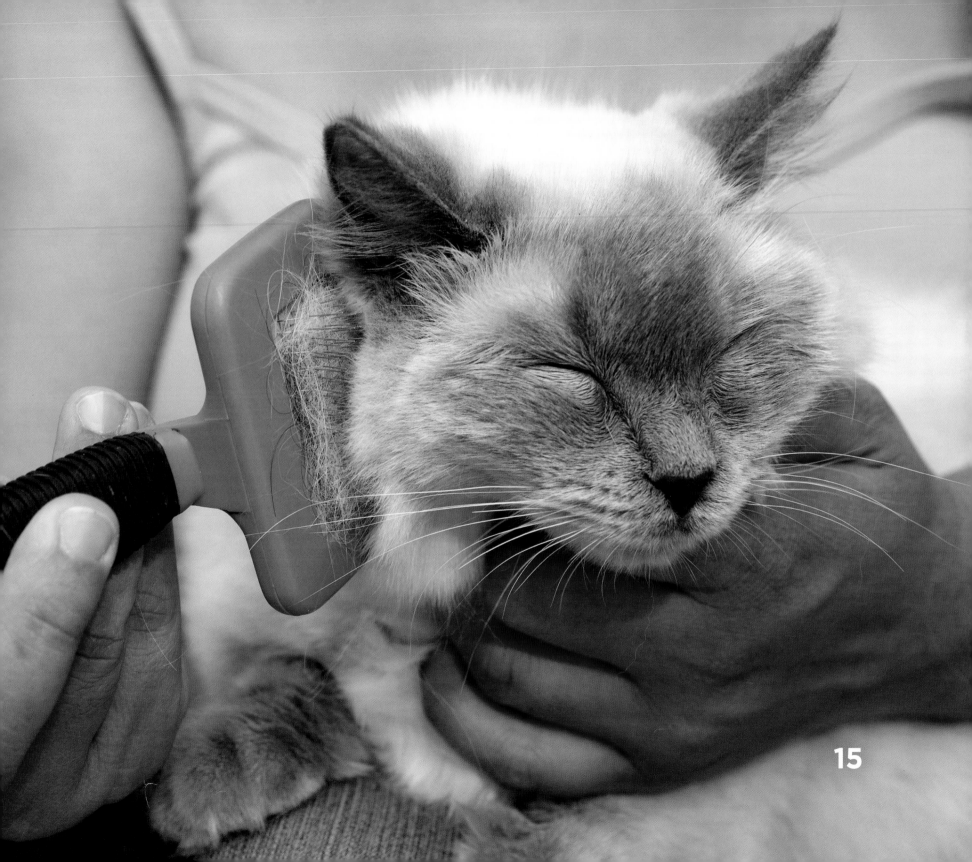

15

Personality & Play

Ragdolls are gentle and kind.

Their **calm** nature makes

them great with kids.

16

17

When they are not snuggling,

they like playing. Many ragdolls

can fetch!

Ragdolls love all people.
They are also happy living
with other animals. This
kind cat is easy to love!

More Facts

- Ragdolls are born all white. Their adult coat colors will begin to show between 8 and 12 weeks old.

- Ragdoll cats take about three years to be fully grown.

- Ragdolls love lots of **affection** and to be held, which is not always the case with other kinds of cats.

Glossary

affection – a gentle feeling of fondness or liking.

calm – not showing or feeling nervousness, anger, or other emotions.

hindquarters – the rear part of an animal.

limp – not firm or stiff.

pattern – a repeated marking.

Index

abdokids.com

Use this code to log on to abdokids.com and access crafts, games, videos and more!

Abdo Kids Code:
CRK9213